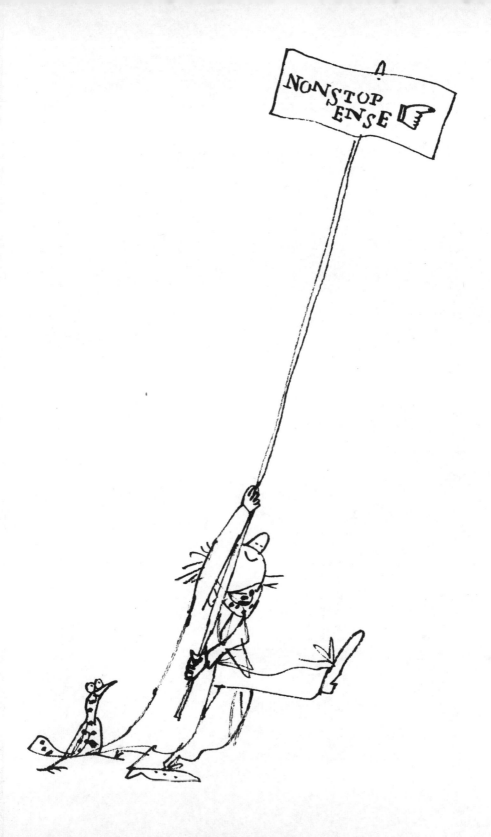

MARGARET MAHY
NONSTOP
NONSENSE
WITH PICTURES BY
QUENTIN BLAKE

J.M. Dent & Sons Ltd
London
Toronto & Melbourne

First published 1977
Text © Margaret Mahy, 1977
Illustrations © Quentin Blake, 1977
Printed in Great Britain by
Biddles Ltd., Guildford, Surrey
J.M. Dent & Sons Limited
Aldine House Albemarle Street London
ISBN 0 460 06806 7

British Library Cataloguing in Publication Data
Mahy, Margaret
 Nonstop nonsense.
 1. Drawings, English
 I. Title II. Blake, Quentin
 823′.9′1J   PZ7.M2773
 ISBN 0–460–06806–7

Contents

The Man from the Land of Fandango

The man from the land of Fandango
Is coming to pay you a call,
With his tri-colour jacket and polka-dot tie
And his calico trousers as blue as the sky
And his hat with a tassel and all.
And he bingles and bangles and bounces,
He's a bird! he's a bell! he's a ball!
The man from the land of Fandango
Is coming to pay you a call.

Oh, whenever they dance in Fandango
The bears and the bison join in,
And baboons with bassoons make a musical sound,
And the kangaroos come with a hop and a bound,
And the dinosaurs join in the din,
And they tingle and tongle and tangle
Till tomorrow turns into today.
Then they stop for a break and a drink and a cake
In their friendly fandandical way.

The man from the land of Fandango
Is given to dancing and dreams.
He comes in at the door like a somersault star
And he juggles with junkets and jam in a jar
And custards and caramel creams.
And he jingles and jongles and jangles
As he dances on ceilings and walls,
And he only appears every five hundred years
So you'd better be home when he calls.

Strange Events in the Life of the Delmonico Family

The Birthday Present

One morning a word wizard was walking home from a successful all-night wizards' party given to open the Monster Sale at the Wizards' Bargain Stores. He heard voices coming through an open window. Mr and Mrs Delmonico were having breakfast and discussing important business. The word wizard, who liked to know about other people's business, stopped and listened carefully.

"Our dear twins are growing up," sighed Mrs Delmonico. "Sarah is so dashing with her beautiful black curls and shining eyes, and Francis is every bit her equal. He says he wants to be an astronomer and study comets. Do you think that is a good career for a boy?"

"I would rather he went into real estate," Mr Delmonico replied. "There is a lot of money in land."

"And what shall we give the twins for their birthday?" Mrs Delmonico went on. "What about a pet of some kind? Children love a pet."

Mr Delmonico did not want his twins, Sarah and Francis to have pets, but he did not like to argue with his wife. He decided to get his own way by cunning.

"What a good idea!" he exclaimed. "I wish I could have ideas like yours, my dear. What sort of pet do you have in mind?"

"A pony perhaps," Mrs Delmonico said doubtfully, but her husband said:

"What a pity! You know I can't stand creatures with eight legs."

"But, Mr Delmonico, my love, horses don't have eight legs. You're thinking of spiders."

"Oh!" said Mr Delmonico rather crossly, "how many legs do they have then?"

"Four each," Mrs Delmonico told him.

Mr Delmonico smiled. "But we'd have to get two ponies — one for Sarah and one for Francis. Two horses with four legs each. That makes eight I'm sure you'll agree, my dear."

"Oh, goodness me, yes, so it does," sighed Mrs Delmonico.

("This man is a very tricky customer!" thought the word wizard listening carefully.)

"Well then, what about a dog?" asked Mrs Delmonico.

"A dog!" muttered Mr Delmonico pretending to consider. "The trouble with dogs is their barking."

"Oh Mr Delmonico, a dog's bark is harmless."

"No," Mr Delmonico replied quickly, "I understand a dog's bark can be worse than his bite, and not only that — dogs are well known for barking up the wrong tree. I don't think a dog would suit this family. We've got so many trees in the garden the poor dog would wear himself out trying to find the right tree to bark up. No. I don't think a dog would do."

"Well, what about a kitten?" asked Mrs Delmonico, crunching toast daintily. "Kittens are pretty and, besides, they're a good investment. Cats have nine lives you know."

"True! True!" answered Mr Delmonico, supping his hot coffee. "But they have their disadvantages. You know how any music on the violin brings on my hay fever."

"But dear, what does a violin have to do with a kitten for the twins?"

"Don't you remember, 'Hey diddle diddle, the cat and the fiddle'?" Mr Delmonico cried.

"But, dear Mr Delmonico, that was only one cat," his wife protested.

"If one can play the fiddle they all can," Mr Delmonico declared. "I don't fancy taking the risk. Besides they're so everyday and all over the place, cats. How about something more unusual?"

"What do you say to a lion, then?" Mrs Delmonico asked. "Lions are very beautiful and very brave. There is a well known saying, 'As bold as a lion'."

"Oh my dear," Mr Delmonico exclaimed laughing, "the real saying is, 'Bald as a lion'. Lions are only beautiful to begin with. On their second birthdays they suddenly go instantaneously bald, and the chairs and the carpets are covered in lion hair."

Mrs Delmonico supped a cup of tea in a disappointed fashion. "I should hate that," she said. "Perhaps we'd better get the twins a pet next year."

"Goodness me, what a woman you are for good ideas," cried Mr Delmonico. "You are very wise, my dear. Leave the twins' birthday presents to me."

("Well," thought the wizard, "here's a man who uses words for the purposes of confustication. Here's a man who chops words and changes meanings. A word wizard can't stand for that. I'll teach him a lesson. Let me see now — what can I contrive?")

The wizard tossed an idea into the air. It buzzed off like a mosquito, over the lawn straight to Mr Delmonico and stung him on the end of his nose.

Mr Delmonico brought his twins, Sarah and Francis presents beginning with "C", like cameras and crayons, clarinets and comics, and a great big fire-engine-red Christmas cracker. It had a black label on it, saying:

"Beware. Monster Cracker."

"I bought it at the Wizards' Bargain Store Monster Sale," Mr Delmonico said. "I can't wait to see what's inside it."

Francis took one end and Sarah took the other. They pulled and they pulled and they pulled and they pulled, and then, suddenly, the cracker burst with a snap and a roar like a cannon let off in a cave full of echoes. The room filled with smoke and the smell of gunpowder.

But when the smoke cleared away there, sitting in the middle of the floor, was a monster.

It had eight legs and carried a violin tucked under its chin. It wore a collar and tie and had a hundred teeth all sharp. It had horns and hairy ears, but the top of its head was quite bald. It smiled at Sarah and Francis and barked.

"A monster! A monster!" cried the twins. "At last we've got a pet. Thank you, thank you, darling father."

Mr Delmonico had to let them keep it, of course, but he couldn't help feeling that someone had got the better of him after all.

The Cat who Became a Poet

A cat once caught a mouse as cats do.

"Don't eat me," cried the mouse. "I am a poet with a poem to write."

"That doesn't make any difference to me," replied the cat. "It is a rule that cats must eat mice and that is all there is to it."

"If only you'd listen to my poem you'd feel differently about it all," said the mouse.

"Okay," yawned the cat, "I don't mind hearing a poem, but I warn you, it won't make any difference."

So the mouse danced and sang:

"The great mouse Night with the starry tail
  Slides over the hills and trees,
  Eating the crumbs in the corners of Day
  And nibbling the moon like cheese."

"Very good! That's very good!" the cat said.
"But a poem is only a poem and cats still eat
mice."

And he ate the mouse, as cats do.

Then he washed his paws and his face and
curled up in a bed of catmint, tucking in his
nose and his tail and his paws. Then he had a
little cat nap.

Some time later he woke up in alarm.

"What's wrong with me?" he thought, "I feel
so strange." He felt as if his head was full of
coloured lights. Pictures came and went behind
his eyes. Things that were different seemed
alike. Things that were real changed and
became dreams.

"Horrakapotchkin!" thought the cat. "I want
to write a poem."

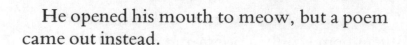

He opened his mouth to meow, but a poem came out instead.

> "The great Sun–Cat comes up in the east.
>   Lo! The glory of his whiskers touches the hills.
>   Behold! the fire of his smiling
>   Burns on the oceans of the rolling world.

"Cat-curses!" said the cat to himself, "I have turned into a poet, but I don't want to make poetry. I just want to be a cat catching mice and sleeping in the catmint bed. I will have to ask the witch about this."

The cat went to the witch's crooked house. The witch sat at the window with her head in her hands. Her dreams turned into black butterflies and flew out of the window.

She took the cat's temperature and gave him some magic medicine that tasted of dandelions.

"Now talk!" she commanded.

The cat opened his mouth to ask her if he was cured. Instead he found himself saying:

> "Lying in the catmint bed,
>   The flowering cherry over my head,
>   Am I really the cat that I seem?
>   Or only a cat in another cat's dream?"

"I'm afraid it is too late," said the witch. "Your case is hopeless. Poetry has got into your blood and you're stuck with it for the rest of your life."

"Horrakapotchkin!" cried the cat sadly and he started off home.

But, five houses away from his own house, a black dog called Max chased him, as dogs do, and the cat had to run up a tree. He boxed with his paw at Max and went to hiss and spit at him, but instead he found himself saying:

"Colonel Dog fires his cannon
And puts his white soldiers on parade.
He guards the house from cats, burglars
And any threat of peacefulness."

The dog Max stopped and stared. "What did you call me? Colonel Dog? I like that. But what do you mean — I fire my cannon?"

"That's your barking" said the cat.

"And what do you mean — I put my white soldiers on parade?" asked the dog again.

26

"That's your teeth," said the cat.

The dog wagged his tail. "I like the way you put it," he said again. "How did you learn to talk like that?"

"Oh, it's poetry," said the cat carelessly. "I am a poet you see."

"Well, I'll tell you what! I'll let you go without barking at you if I may come and hear that poem again sometimes," the dog Max said, still wagging his tail. "Perhaps I could bring some other dogs to hear it too. Colonel Dog, eh? White soldiers eh? Very true." And he let the cat go on home to his catmint bed.

"If only he knew," the cat thought. "I wasn't meaning to praise him. Poetry is very tricky stuff and can be taken two ways."

The cat went on thinking. "I became a poet through eating the mouse. Perhaps the mouse became a poet through eating seeds. Perhaps all this poetry stuff is just the world's way of talking about itself." And straight away he felt another poem coming into his mind.

"Just time for a sleep first," he muttered into his whiskers. "One thing, I'll never eat another poet again. One is quite enough." And he curled up in the catmint bed for a quick kip-and-catnap as cats do.

Let's get to the next page before he wakes up...

George's Pet

When George and his gorilla
Go bounding down the street,
They get respectful nods and smiles
From neighbours that they meet.

If George had owned a puppy dog,
Or else a kitty-cat,
His neighbours wouldn't notice him
With courtesy like that.

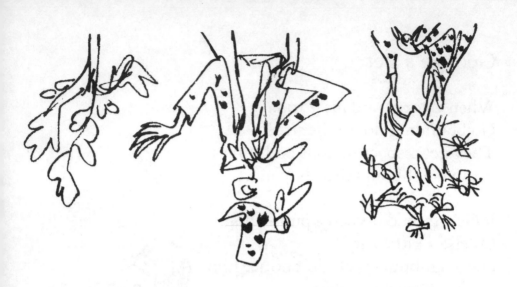

Why Anna Hung Upside Down

One day Anna, wearing her blue jeans, went
out and climbed onto the first branch of the
second tree to the right of the supermarket.

Then she hung by her knees.

She saw the world upside down. The grass was
the sky and the sky was the grass. The supermarket
poured people upwards into the green air.

An old man with a ridiculous hat came by.

"Look at this girl," he said to a thin woman
with fluffy slippers and curlers. "She's upside
down."

"My goodness so she is!" the thin woman
cried. "Why do you think that's happened?"

"I don't know," the man replied. "Perhaps
it's the weather, we've had some funny weather
lately and it may be affecting the children."

"Perhaps she's doing it for health reasons," said a sickly looking goat. "Being upside down lets the blood into the brain, and that perks you up no end."

A lion and a School Inspector going home from the supermarket stopped to look on curiously. The lion said nothing, but the School Inspector said: "It's the parents' fault. Parents let their children do anything these days. Now this poor child's parents are most likely at home drinking tea and reading the paper and not looking after their girl. *They* don't care that she's gone all upside down out here."

"Yes, that's right!" called the mother of twins. "They don't care at all. Now if my twins were to go all upside down like that, I'd smack them with the hair brush. That'd bring them right way up again pretty quick I can tell you."

At this point, a boy called Ron, oldest of five, climbed up into the tree too and hung beside Anna.

"Look at that, now there's two of them at it," cried an excited voice, probably a hen. There were quite a few hens in the crowd.

"It's catching, it's catching," shouted the thin woman in fluffy slippers and the crowd moved back several steps nervously.

"I don't want to go upside down," whimpered a rich man. "All my money would fall out of my pockets."

"Neither you shall!" said his pretty secretary, hurrying him away and looking angrily at Anna and Ron as she went.

"It's the new craze," said a folk-singing crocodile strumming on her guitar. Then she sang showing long rows of well-kept teeth:

"Upside down — upside down ——
The newest craze to hit the town . . ."

But at this point a little girl called Sally wearing a track suit climbed into the tree and hung by her knees next to Ron.

"I still say it's the weather!" cried the man in the ridiculous hat.

"Now then," said a policeman coming up. "What's all this?"

"Look, look, the police have come," twittered some excitable guinea pigs, and a small number of culprits and criminals slunk away to evade the eye of the law.

"These poor children, neglected by their parents, have gone all upside down," said the School Inspector in an important voice.

"But perhaps," suggested a Professor of Philosophy going by with a meat pie in a paper bag, "perhaps they are the right way up. Perhaps it is we who are upside down."

This upset a lot of people. There was a resentful muttering and the sound of gritting teeth.

The policeman had to do something quickly. People and animals were all upset. He thought hard.

"Send for the fire brigade," he commanded at last.

But the lion who had been watching thoughtfully, said in a deep lion's voice, "Ask them! Ask them why they are hanging upside down."

The policeman came up to Anna. "Now then, young lady!" he said, "why are you upside down in that tree?"

"I learned to do this yesterday," replied Anna, "I just wanted to see if I could still do it today."

"It's fun!" shouted Ron. "You all look funny upside down."

And Sally shouted: "Upside down frowns turn into smiles."

Then Anna put up her hands and swung down from the branch, and so did Ron and Sally.

"Why are you doing that?" asked the man in the ridiculous hat.

"Well, the bend of my knees is starting to hurt a bit," Anna said. "And not only that, it's dinner time and hanging upside down makes you hungry. Are you coming?" And then all three walked away leaving the first branch of the second tree to the right of the supermarket absolutely empty.

Foolish frog

The Remarkable Cake

It's Christmas — the time when we gather to make
A truly remarkable once-a-year cake.
The recipe's written in letters of gold
By a family witch who is terribly old.

The rule of this cakc is it has to be made
In a wheelbarrow (stirred with a shovel or spade)
At Christmas, the season of love and good will.
Other times of the year it might make you feel ill.

You must nail it together or stick it with glue,
Then hammer it flat with the heel of your shoe.
You must stretch it out thin, you must tie it in knots,
Then get out your paint box and paint it with spots.

What a taste! What a flavour! It's certain to please.
It's rather like ice cream with pickles and cheese.
In June it would taste like spaghetti and mud,
While its taste in September would curdle your blood.

Oh, what a cake! It looks simply delicious.
Now get out the carving knife, get out the dishes!
Be careful! Be careful! This cake might explode,
And blow up the kitchen and part of the road.

Oh dear! It's exploded! I thought that it might.
It's not very often we get it just right.
Let's comfort the baby, revive Uncle Dan,
And we'll start it all over as soon as we can.

For Christmas — that gipsy day — comes and it goes
Far sooner than ever we dare to suppose.
Once more in December we'll gather to make
That truly remarkable once-a-year cake.

Fair Exchange

Mr Salt had two sayings.

One was — Fair exchange is no robbery — and the other was — A man needs his sleep.

The seven Salt children were as sharp as needles and as bright as pins, and Mr Salt himself could sing songs of sad lovers or tell tales of mystery and adventure. However his main hobby was sleeping. While he slept the house got older and older and began to fall to pieces. Water came in like an invited guest, and so did Mr Salt's wild hungry hens who thought that the Salt's house was full of delicious food. Hens are usually timid, but Mr Salt's hens feared neither man nor beast.

Jeremy Salt, the oldest Salt child, complained to his father about the house tumbling down and the hens coming in, but all Mr Salt would say was: "Only the house! Only the hens! Oh, let me sleep again," and start a melodious but manly snoring that made Jeremy feel guilty about waking him in the first place.

However, one morning when the snoring started, Jeremy shook his father and woke him again.

"Is it the end of the world?" asked Mr Salt, opening eyes as blue as periwinkles for the second time that morning.

"No Dad, no! Just listen! A window's come out and a door's fallen in and the hens are all over the kitchen. They've pecked the cat and the baby. Can't you build a hen run, Dad, so the hens will stay put?"

"Goodness me!" cried Mr Salt. "If only your dear mother were alive. There was a woman who could have had a hen run up in a flash. Oh well — I've done a bit of building in my time. Bring me the hammer and bring me the nails and bring me some two by two."

"What's two by two Daddy?" asked one of the seven little Salts — a girl one.

"It's a size of wood my dear, a very famous size, two inches this way and two inches that . . . it's what Noah built the ark out of."

"The ark Daddy?"

"Yes, my dear — haven't you heard the animals went in two by two? Now you get to work and bring me some two by two too."

The Salt children bought a little and borrowed a little and carried it to the other end of the garden. The hens watched them out of small yellow eyes, each hen standing on one leg with curiosity.

"Carry Dad down to the end of the section. Don't make him walk or he'll be tired out," said Jeremy. The seven little Salts pushed and pulled Mr Salt's bed down to the other end of the garden. Mr Salt opened one eye and saw the

hammer, saw the nails, saw the two by two.

"Get to work, my darlings," he whispered. "You can do it if you try. I'll give you a few clues."

In between yawns Mr Salt told his children where to saw and where to hammer and which end of the nail came first.

"Make it big," he commanded. "Those hens are used to the freedom of the hedge. I don't want them to be miserable."

As the hen house grew bigger and bigger the children became more and more interested.

They painted the door blue and the roof red.
They put up window boxes full of wild flowers
— yarrow, mayweed, plantain and pimpernel.
They made a lovely long hen run, with two by
two and chicken wire. At last they were
finished. Then the little Salts looked at the new
hen house and sighed.

"What a beautiful house!" they said to one
another. "Daddy, may we get our little chairs
and sit in the house for a while before we put the
hens in it?"

"A good idea," Mr Salt declared. "Push my
bed in too. I'm all worn out with mental
activity and I'll have a little nap in the shade."

Looking out from the hen house the little
Salts saw the world quite differently. From this
end of the garden they could look between the
hills and see the blue waters of the sea. As the
sun set, the blue turned to gold and the hills
were edged with scarlet.

"Daddy, may we bring down our big bed
and the patchwork quilt and sleep in the hen
house all night?" asked the little Salts.

"Certainly, my dears," replied Mr Salt,
between breathing in and breathing out.

So the little Salts brought down their big bed
and their patchwork quilt and slept all night in
the new hen house.

In the morning there were no hens to scratch on the doormat and peck at the floor. They were all up at the big house wondering where the Salt family had got to. And even when they found them, they couldn't get at them, because the hen run, made for keeping the hens in, was also very good at keeping them out, so the baby could eat her biscuit in peace without any fear that a hen might snatch it out of pure greed and malice.

"Oh father!" said the little Salts. "Let the hens have our old house and let us live in the nice new hen house."

"A good idea!" said Mr Salt. "Fair exchange is no robbery. Besides, having got this far, I doubt if I have the strength to move back again. After all a man does need his sleep, you know."

So the Salt family lived in the hen house with the blue door and the hens lived in the Salts' old house. Pieces kept on dropping off the old house and the view wasn't very good, but the hens didn't mind and laid just as many eggs as if they too could watch the sea turn golden in the evening, or silver by the light of the moon.

My Sister

My sister's remarkably light,
She can float to a fabulous height.
It's a troublesome thing,
But we tie her with string,
And we use her instead of a kite.

Circles

Two loaves of bread are very well,
One to eat and one to sell.
With the money that I get
I buy a bird to be my pet.

Eating bread like any king
I hear the bird begin to sing.
Catch the song without delay ——
Quick, before it flies away.

Getting paper, pen and ink,
Sit and dream and sit and think.
Quickly catch in net of words
Taste of bread and song of birds.

46

Take the poem I have made,
(Quite a long one, I'm afraid),
Rush to clever printing man,
Sell the poem if I can.

Ring the merry money bell!
(Doesn't money jingle well?)
Bored with money, buy instead
Two good loaves of crusty bread.

Two loaves of bread are very well
One to eat and one to sell.
One to sell and buy — who knows —
A silver fish or flowering rose.

Strange Events in the Life of the Delmonico Family

Trouble in the Supermarket

One day when he was in a very joking mood Mr Delmonico offended a word witch. He did it by being a bit too clever. (Too much cleverness is often offensive to witches.)

Mr Delmonico, with his twins, Francis and Sarah, was shopping at the supermarket. The witch was there too, pushing a shopping trolley and talking to herself as word witches do . . . they need a lot of words going on around them all the time.

"I'll have some peanut butter," she said.

"You'd butter not," cried Mr Delmonico, laughing at his own joke. The word witch took no notice, just went on talking to herself.

"And then perhaps I'll have a loaf of wholemeal bread," she went on.

Mr Delmonico winked at the twins. "How can you make a meal out of a hole?" he asked. "It doesn't sound very nice."

Francis and Sarah were horrified to hear their father speaking so carelessly to a word witch. But the witch ignored him. She was trying hard to behave well in a public place.

"I'll get some beans," she muttered.

Mr Delmonico looked at the beans. He couldn't resist another joke. "They look more like 'might-have beans'," he remarked with a smile.

Now the witch turned on him, glaring with her small red eyes. "I've had quite enough of you," she cried. "You shall suffer from whirling words and see how you like it."

Mr Delmonico was suddenly serious as the word witch scuttled away.

Whirling words sounded as if they might be painful.

"I'm afraid I might have got us into a bit of a jam," he said to the twins.

"Daddy, be careful," cried Sarah, but it was too late. They were up to their ankles in several kinds of jam. Francis was mainly mixed up with strawberry, Sarah with plum and apple, while Mr Delmonico himself had melon and ginger jam up over the turn-ups of his trousers. The manager of the supermarket came hurrying up.

"What's going on here?" he cried.

"Nothing really," Mr Delmonico said, trying to sound casual. "Just some jam that was lying around."

"There's something fishy about this," declared the manager and then gasped, for a large flapping fish appeared out of nowhere and struck him on the right ear. Sarah and Francis realized that anyone near Mr Delmonico was going to suffer from whirling words too.

"You are to blame for all this mess," said the manager, "and you'll have to pay for it."

"Oh, will I!" replied Mr Delmonico, trying hard to keep calm. "Wait till I ring my lawyer."

An elegant gold ring with an enormous diamond in it appeared in his hand. Mr Delmonico looked guilty and tried to hide it behind the bottles of vinegar. "You can do what you like, you'll have to pay," said the manager.

"*Me? Pay?* Look at my trousers all over jam! I shall lose my temper in a moment. You're just egging me on."

Eggs began to fall out of the air. A few of them hit the supermarket manager, but most of them broke on Mr Delmonico. He was jam to the knees and egg to the ears.

"Stop it!" cried the manager. "And you talk of lawyers — why, you haven't got a leg to stand on."

Mr Delmonico sat down suddenly in the jam.

"We must get out of this before the balloon goes up," whispered Francis to Sarah, and he found himself rising out of the jam, Sarah beside him. To their delight a beautiful air balloon was carrying them gently away.

"Quick!" said Francis. "Grab Dad."

Catching Mr Delmonico by the collar and by the belt of his trousers his clever twins hoisted him into the air.

The manager waved his fist at them and shouted: "You haven't heard the last of this."

The balloon swooped through the supermarket door and skimmed over the roofs of the town.

"Home!" ordered Mr Delmonico. "I'm not going to *that* shop again. They have a very funny way of displaying fish and jam."

Francis shook his head. "You shouldn't have teased the word witch, Dad."

"Oh, these word witches need to be teased," Mr Delmonico replied grandly, "wispy creatures with their heads in the clouds — whereas I am a pretty down to earth fellow."

At that moment Mr Delmonico's collar and trouser belt gave way and he fell to earth — fortunately into his very own garden which he had dug and raked that morning until it was as soft as velvet.

"We're home," said Francis, "but the whirling words are still with us. What will we do about that?"

Harry the Hawk

Harry the Hawk on his magic trapeze
Flies over the roofs of the city with ease.
He hangs by his heels and he swings by his knees.
Tumultuous Harry the Hawk.

He has the grand acrobatical style.
Stop when you see him and watch for a while.
He has a secret tucked into his smile.
Mysterious Harry the Hawk.

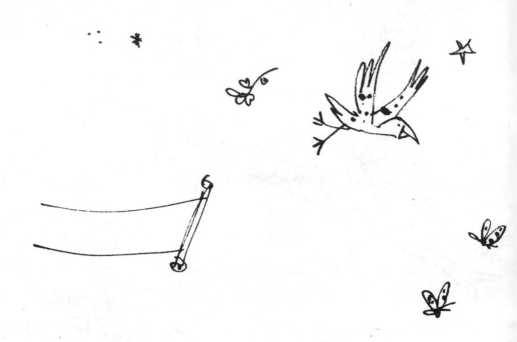

If he should fall, there's no need for dismay,
He'll just give a laugh that is gallant and gay.
Spreading his wings, he'll go floating away.
That's why he's Harry the Hawk,

Bird boy with never a fret or a care,
Woven of sunshine and warm summer air,
Sparrows and stars in the net of his hair.
FANTASTICAL Harry the Hawk.

What I Like . . .

What I like for dinner when I'm on my own
Is Fish and Chips, Asparagus tips,
And an ice-cream cone.

What I like for dinner when I have a guest
Is Mossy Fudge, and Muddly Sludge,
And baked Bird's Nest.

The Tarragon Vinegar Song

Only the best and the finest ingredients
Do for a song that is written for you.
Ravenous uncles and many thin greedy aunts
Yearn for the music so lively and new.
"What did you put in this song?" they all say,
"To make it turn out this exotical way?"

Tarragon, tarragon, tarragon vinegar,
Bubble-cake-custard and blueberry ice,
Butterfly bacon and cutlet of crocodile,
Make up a mixture worth double the price.

Kings and their courtiers come to investigate,
Queens in kimonos consistently call,
Presidents knock on the east or the westi-gate,
Princes on ponies jump over the wall.
"Oh, are you a man from the echoless moon
That you play this fantastamalogical tune?"

Tarragon, tarragon, tarragon vinegar,
Willow leaves, whiskers and waterfall wine,
Potpourri pancakes and cream of the dandelion,
Make up a melody friendly and fine.

For they all love the music — relations and royalty,
Lawyer and layabout, doctor and nurse.
A thief tried to steal it. His plans were all spoilt. He
'S now just a line in the very last verse.
He is trapped by the words, but he constantly hears
The harmonious hum of the heavenly spheres.

Tarragon, tarragon, tarragon vinegar,
Oceans are heard in the heart of a shell.
Hippos and harlequins join in a harmony
Kings in their crowns cannot conquer or quell.

The Insect Kingdom that didn't get Started

There are seven hundred thousand different sorts of insects, and once there was very nearly a wonderful insect kingdom full of insects who understood one another and were loving and kind. It happened like this.

A spider caught a fly in her web and was just going to wrap him up like a school lunch when a woman vacuuming, sucked the spider, the fly, the cobweb and all, into the vacuum cleaner.

The spider pulled her legs in tight so as not to lose any. She was whirled round and round down a long black tunnel until at last she reached a place where all was dark and soft and dusty. There was a roaring noise in the air, but the whirling had stopped. The spider looked with all her eight eyes, but she could not see a single thing. She couldn't think what had happened.

At last the woman switched off the vacuum cleaner and all was quiet.

"Help!" the spider called. "Help! Help!"

"Who's that calling 'Help!'?" asked a voice almost in her ear.

"It's me, a poor spider," the spider replied. "Who is there?"

"Oh, it's you, spider baby," said the voice. "I'm a fly you were going to eat, just a few minutes ago. We're both in this thing together."

"Oh!" cried the spider, "am I glad to hear you! What's happened do you suppose? Is it the end of the world?"

"Heck no!" said the fly carelessly. "We've just been eaten by something bigger than both of us. That's the way things are. Spiders eat flies, birds eat spiders, cats eat birds. It's either eat or get eaten in this life."

The spider was silent for a while.

"I didn't think it would end like this," she said at last. "Now I feel sorry for all the flies I've eaten in the past. If only I could get out of here I'd live my life differently, I can tell you."

"Funny you should say that," said the fly. "I was thinking the same thing. If only I could have my time over again, I'd be a different fly. I'd stay away from rubbish heaps and I'd never walk all over someone's meat with dirty shoes on again."

"I'd learn to eat berries," the spider declared. "I'd drink honey like a butterfly. I'm not really an insect myself, but I'd learn insect ways."

"Come to think, spider baby," the fly said. "I don't suppose a fly and a spider ever had a chance to understand each other's point of view before. We've never had the chance to talk together as we're talking now."

"And to think the chance should have come too late," the spider wept. "Why, if we'd known then what we know now, we could have changed the world."

And they went on talking together in the smothering darkness of the vacuum cleaner bag, dreaming of what might have been, sobbing and moaning, "Too late! Too late!" and "If only we had a second chance." They dreamed of a wonderful kingdom where spiders and insects understood each other and were loving and kind. Then the woman came back from her lunch and emptied the bag of dust onto the compost heap.

"This is it!" cried the fly as they were taken and shaken up and down. "This is it, spider baby." Dust, pieces of paper, breadcrumbs, scraps of orange peel, pins, threads and fluff swelled and swirled pellmell, holus bolus around them.

"Too late, dear fly, too late," the spider replied faintly.

But it wasn't too late! When the spider recovered from her faint she found herself

bruised, but otherwise well and strong, on the
compost heap. She stretched her legs. They
were all there. She set to work and made a new
web. Just as she finished it she saw a fly sitting
on a leaf, cleaning his wings with his hind legs
and watching her.

"Is that you, dear fly?" she asked hopefully.

"Is that you, spider baby?" replied the fly.

"I've just finished making the prettiest web,"
the spider went on. "It's a new sort of peaceful
web. Come and see it."

"It looks a lot like the last one," the fly replied. "I think I'll stay here."

"But fly — we're friends now," the spider pleaded. "All the wicked past is forgotten. Don't you remember our plans, our dreams?"

"I haven't forgotten," the fly replied. "But it doesn't seem as important now as it did then. I mean, like, it was dark and dusty then, and it's bright and sunny now. And I am a fly and, after all, spider baby, you *are* a spider. I'm off."

"Where are you going?" shrieked the spider.

"Off to find a good dirty rubbish heap, and then to walk all over someone's lunch in my dirty boots," the fly replied and he flew away.

The spider hung herself head downwards in the exact centre of her new web.

"It's terrible the way some people forget their dreams of better things. There are not many people prepared to struggle for a better world. And he was so fat and delicious looking too. Never mind. There'll be another one along soon."

And that is how the kingdom of the insects didn't get started after all. Aren't we lucky, you and I, that we would have more sense than that.

Unexpected Summer Soup

I drank some soup this afternoon,
And what do you think I found in my spoon?
    Onions and Peas!
Of course I didn't mind.
It's what you'd expect to find.

I drank some soup this afternoon,
And what do you think I found in my spoon?
    Onions and Peas,
      A Hive of Bees . . .
Oh, what a surprise!
I couldn't believe my eyes.

I drank some soup this afternoon,
And what do you think I found in my spoon?
    Onions and Peas,
    A Hive of Bees,
    A Crown, a Carrot . . .
Oh, shivers and shocks!
I nearly jumped out of my socks.

I drank some soup this afternoon,
And what do you think I found in my spoon?
    Onions and Peas,
    A Hive of Bees,
    A Crown, a Carrot,
    A Patchwork Parrot . . .
A-ghast, a-gape, a-gog,
I nearly stood on the dog.

I drank some soup this afternoon,
And what do you think I found in my spoon?
    Onions and Peas,
    A Hive of Bees,
    A Crown, a Carrot,
    A Patchwork Parrot,
    A Sprig of Sage . . .
I didn't choose to object,
It's what you might expect.

I drank some soup this afternoon,
And what do you think I found in my spoon?
     Onions and Peas,
     A Hive of Bees,
     A Crown, a Carrot,
     A Patchwork Parrot,
     A Sprig of Sage,
     A Frog in a Cage . . .
What do you say to that?
It certainly scared the cat.

I drank some soup this afternoon,
And what do you think I found in my spoon?
     Onions and Peas,
     A Hive of Bees,
     A Crown, a Carrot,
     A Patchwork Parrot,
     A Sprig of Sage,
     A Frog in a Cage,
     A Witch's Shoe . . .
Taken unaware,
I tumbled off my chair.

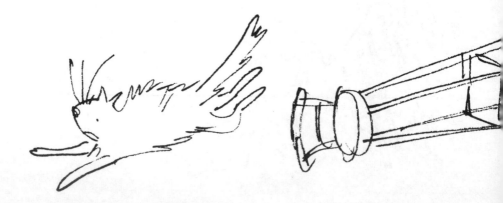

I drank some soup this afternoon,
And what do you think I found in my spoon?
      Onions and Peas,
      A Hive of Bees,
      A Crown, a Carrot,
      A Patchwork Parrot,
      A Sprig of Sage,
      A Frog in a Cage,
      A Witch's Shoe,
      And a Mermaid too
Who sang a song so sweet and shrill
That the summery day outside stood still.

I asked my mother where she sat,
"How do you make a soup like that?"
"You have to gather, you have to guard,
Things odd and even, striped and starred,
All the dark things, all the light,
That come to your door by day or night,
It isn't easy at all, my dear,
But I'll make it again another year,
With . . .

     Onions and Peas,
     A Hive of Bees,
     A Crown, a Carrot,
     A Patchwork Parrot,
     A Sprig of Sage,
     A Frog in a Cage,
     A Witch's Shoe,
     And a Mermaid too . . .

A Song, a Story, and anything more
That a summer wind brings to my door."

Strange Events in the Life of the Delmonico Family

Phone Talk

The same evening after their adventure at the supermarket Francis and Sarah Delmonico were doing their homework quietly by the fire when the telephone rang.

"Don't move! I'll get it," called Mrs Delmonico, and she glided daintily across the room to pick up the phone. Francis and Sarah listened curiously.

"Oh, is that you, Coral?" Mrs Delmonico piped happily. Coral was a friend of hers who played a good game of golf. "How nice to hear from you just when I'm feeling a little blue."

Now Sarah and Francis noticed a very strange thing happen when their mother said this. She turned blue — just a pale blue at first, but getting brighter until she was the colour of the stripes in a butcher's apron, rather a strong navy.

"No, no — I'm perfectly well," she went on. "Really I'm in the pink of condition." At once the blue took on a purply tinge and then slowly changed to a lovely soft sunset pink. Francis and Sarah stared in astonishment.

"No, it's just that it's been raining so much that I haven't been able to get into the garden," Mrs Delmonico explained. "I love the garden

you know. Things grow for me because I've
got green fingers." Mrs Delmonico twiddled
the fingers of her left hand in the air as she spoke
but she wasn't looking at them. They turned a
bright green. It looked as if her hand had
sprouted blades of grass.

"More word trouble," Sarah sighed. "Words
in our house are like acrobats, twisting and
tumbling all over the place."

"Listen," commanded Francis.

"Yes, yes!" Mrs Delmonico was saying. "I
heard about that. Really what will the commit-
tee get up to next. It makes me see red to think
about it." Mrs Delmonico's face stayed pink
and her fingers stayed green but her eyes grew
bright red like little coals of fire. It was a very

disconcerting effect indeed. Mr Delmonico, coming in from the kitchen, a tea towel in his hand, was certainly surprised to see his wife so changed. But Mrs Delmonico went on talking. She had begun to talk about Mr Delmonico.

"Oh, he's well," she said gaily, "only a bit browned off at present." Mr Delmonico turned a handsome mahogany brown, nice and shiny, as if he had been well polished. "Work, work, work!" Mrs Delmonico chattered on. "But business is good. Everything he touches turns to gold at present." Mr Delmonico caught sight of himself in the mirror over the fireplace and his mouth opened in horror. But then his anxious eyes switched to the tea towel in his hand. It turned a dull yellow, grew heavy and hard to hold. Francis and Sarah knew that Mr Delmonico had turned into a sort of King Midas. Everything he touched was turning to gold. When he pulled out his handkerchief to rub his glossy brown face . . . lo and behold! the handkerchief was golden before it reached his troubled brow.

"Look here. . ." cried Mr Delmonico in a peevish voice, but Mrs Delmonico, talking happily, did not hear him.

"His brothers and sisters don't know what to say. They get very jealous at times — but of course, he's always been the black sheep of the family."

80

Wool, black curly wool, began to appear on Mr Delmonico's head. His ears grew larger and his face grew longer. He began to turn into a sheep.

"Baaaaa!" cried Mr Delmonico despairingly.

"What can we do?" asked Sarah in great agitation.

"Think of something quickly," Francis replied. "Get her to say something dull and ordinary. But I don't know what. It's all too much for me . . . ."

But things weren't too much for Mrs Delmonico.

"Me?" she said over the phone. "Oh no, I'm not a colourful sort of person myself — totally colourless, in fact." Her red eyes, pink face and green fingers began to fade back to ordinary person-colour. "Everything that happens around me is very ordinary," Mrs Delmonico said, laughing lightly. "Ordinary, average and humdrum!" Mr Delmonico began to look more like his ordinary average and humdrum self and so did the tea towel and the handkerchief. Mr Delmonico stared at them and then at his reflection in the mirror.

"It must have been a dream," he said aloud so that Sarah and Francis could hear him. "But I'm not wearing my pyjamas. Funny things have been happening today and it seems as if this might be another one of them."

"What might be another one of what?" asked Mrs Delmonico who had just put the phone down because Coral's soup was boiling over, and she had to rush away.

"Just for a moment there, I felt most peculiar," Mr Delmonico answered. "But now I'm seeing things in their true colours."

"My poor dear," Mrs Delmonico said. "Sit down! I'll bring you a lovely glass of cold fizzy lemonade. Because, now I come to look at you, Mr Delmonico darling, you're looking very green about the gills. Oh! Oh dear! What's wrong with the man?" For Mr Delmonico had fainted away.

So watch your language, friend

Sensible Questions

"Suppose the land turned into the sea?"
"Don't be stupid! It couldn't be!"

"Suppose the sea turned into the land?"
"It wouldn't happen. You don't understand!"

"Suppose I waved his grassy stalk,
And Max the dog began to talk?"

"Your fancy's foolish. Your ways are wild!
I often think you're a silly child!"

83

But Marigold waved her stalk of grass
And all she had asked about came to pass.

The land rolled up and the sea rolled over
The waves were covered with grass and clover,

While Marigold and her reproving aunt
Who'd kept on saying "Don't!" and "Can't!",

Were up to their necks in a wild green sea —
And Max the dog said, "Fiddle dee dee!"

The Haunted Child

Oh, I am haunted at my play
And haunted in my bed,
But does the spirit haunt the house
Or does it haunt my head?

It mutters often in my ear . . .
I know when it's about,
But is it whispering to get in
Or weeping to get out?

The outside rooms, these painted walls
Where I am washed and fed
Are nothing but the shadows cast
By rooms inside my head.

And in the house behind my eyes
I watch the world go by
Strong as a king until I hear
That thin and needling cry.

All shadows, shades and wicked imps,
All creatures of the gloom,
And pucks and pixies may appear
Haunting my outside room.

But oh, but oh, my inside rooms!
Let no ghosts wander there,
And Silence be the only guest
Between my chin and hair.

The Reluctant Hero
or
Barefoot in the Snow

When he put on his socks in the morning
He found they were much too tight.
His feet, without any warning,
Had lengthened over night.
He didn't have any others,
He couldn't pick or choose.
He borrowed a pair of his mother's
And went to put on his shoes.

When he put on his shoes in the morning
He found they were much too tight.
His feet, without any warning,
Had lengthened in the night.
His toes and heels were skinned — oh,
His feet had grown like roots.
His shoes went out of the window
And he went to put on his boots.

When he put on his boots in the morning
He found they were much too tight.
His feet, without any warning,
Had lengthened over night.
His little toe was just in,
He had to squash and squeeze.
He threw them into the dust bin
And he went to put on his skis.

When he put on his skis in the morning
He found they were much too tight.
His feet, without any warning,
Had lengthened over night.
He had no footware which in
His feet could feel at ease.
The skis went into the kitchen
And his toes were left to freeze.

And so he went out barefoot,
No socks or shoes he wore.
He trod in places where foot
Had never trod before.
And everywhere his feet sent
A message to the sky.
His footprints down the street meant
A hero's passing by.

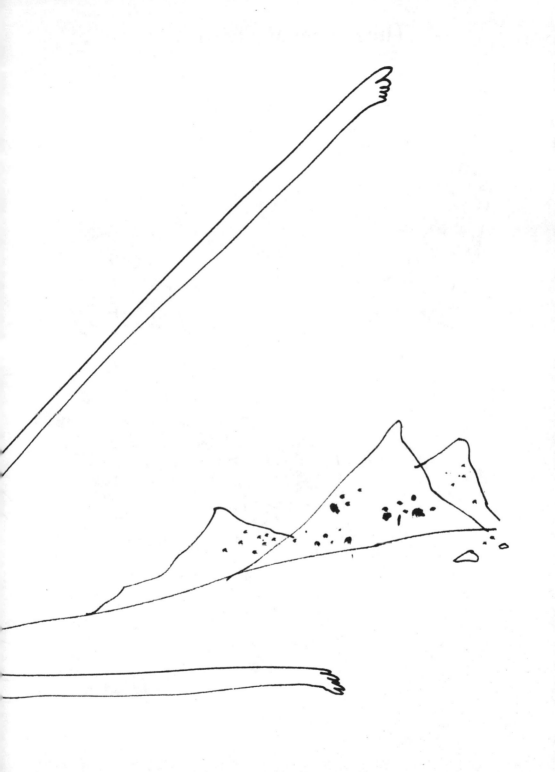

The Dictionary Bird

Through my house in sunny weather
Flies the Dictionary Bird
Clear to see on every feather
Is some outlandish word.

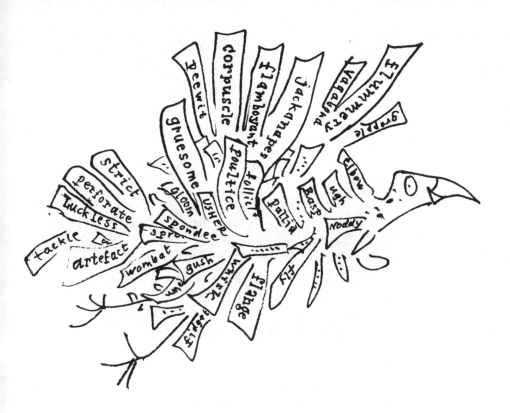

"Hugger Mugger" "gimcrack" "guava"
"Waggish" "mizzle" "swashing rain"
Bird—fly back into my kitchen,
Let me read those words again.

The Ghost who Came out of the Book

There was once a very small ghost who lived in a book — a book of ghost stories, of course. Sometimes people caught a glimpse of it and thought it was some sort of book mark, but mostly people did not see it at all. When anybody opened the book to read it the ghost slipped out from between the pages and flew around the room, looking at the people and the people's things. Then, when the ghost saw that the person reading the book was growing sleepy or was finishing the story, it slid back into the book and hid between the pages again. There was one page it especially liked with a picture of a haunted house on it.

One evening a child was reading the ghost stories and the ghost slipped out of the book as usual. It flew around the top of the room and looked at spiders' webs in the corners of the ceiling. It tugged at the webs and the spiders came out thinking they'd caught something. Then the very small ghost shouted "Boo!" at them, frightening them so that they ran back into their cracks and corners to hide. While the ghost was doing this, the child's mother came in, shut the book, kissed the child and put the light out all in a second or two. The ghost was

shut out of the book and left outside in the world of the house.

"Oh well," said the ghost, quite pleased, "a good chance to try some haunting on a larger scale. I'm getting a bit sick of spiders anyway."

The door was shut with an iron catch so the ghost couldn't get into the rest of the house. It just flew around the bedroom a few times and went to sleep at last in the folds of the curtains, hanging upside down like a bat.

"What a day to look forward to tomorrow!" it thought happily just before it went to sleep. "I'll scare everyone in the place. I might not bother to go back to the book again."

But alas, the next morning the ghost slept in.

The mother of the house came in briskly and flicked the curtains wide. The ghost, taken by surprise, broke into two or three pieces and had to join up again.

"There's a cobweb up there," the mother of the house said, and before the ghost was properly joined up again she vacuumed it into her vacuum cleaner. Of course, a vacuum cleaner was nothing to a ghost. This ghost just drifted straight out again, but it certainly felt shaken and there was dust all the way through it.

"Now I am getting very angry," the ghost said to itself, and it followed the mother of the house into the kitchen and hissed a small buzzing hiss into her ear.

"Goodness, there's a fly in the kitchen," said the mother, and she took out the fly spray and squirted it in the direction of the hiss.

Being a ghost, this ghost didn't breathe, but the fly spray made it get pins and needles all over and it went zigging and zagging about the kitchen looking like a piece of cobweb blown about the kitchen by a playful breeze. At last it settled on the refrigerator.

"I'll just take things quietly for a bit," the

ghost whispered to itself. "Things are getting too much for me." It watched the mother dust the window ledges.

"Why does she do that?" the ghost wondered, for the dust looked like speckles of gold and silver and freckles of rainbow. Some dots of dust were like tiny glass wheels with even tinier glass wheels spinning inside them. Some specks were whole worlds with strange islands and mysterious oceans on them, but all too small, too small for anyone but a very small ghost to see.

But when the mother began to make a cake the ghost gasped, for she poured in a measure of sugar that looked like thousands of ice diamonds all spangled and sparkling with white and blue and green. "Let me have a closer look at them," the ghost murmured to itself, and it flew down into the sugar. At that moment the mother of the house began to beat the cake mixture with her electric egg beater.

"Help!" screamed the ghost as it was whirled into the sugar and butter and got runny egg all over it.

The cake mixture was so sticky that the ghost got rather glued up in it, and before it knew what was happening it was poured into a greased tin and put into the oven. Being a ghost, nothing dangerous could happen to it. In fact the warmth of the oven was soothing and the ghost yawned and decided, as things were so unexpected and alarming outside, to stay where it was. It curled up in the centre of the cake and went to sleep.

It did not wake up until tea time. Then it heard voices.

"Oh boy — cake!" it heard the voices say.

"Yes," said the mother of the house, "I made it this morning." And in the next moment a knife came down and cut the ghost in two. It joined up again at once, and when the slice was lifted out of the cake the ghost leaped out too,

waving in the air like a cobweb and shouting,
"Boo!"

"Oh!" cried the children. "A ghost! A ghost!
The cake's haunted."

"Nonsense — just a bit of steam," said the
mother firmly, touching the cake with the back
of her hand. "Funny thing though — it's quite
cool."

"Perhaps it's a sort of volcano cake," the
father suggested. "Never mind! It tastes
lovely."

"It tastes haunted!" the children told each
other, for they were clever enough to taste the
ghost taste in between the raisins, a little bit
sharp and sour like lemon juice.

The ghost meanwhile flew back to the bed-room where the book lived.

"First the whirlwind and then the desert," it said to itself, thinking of the vacuum cleaner and the vacuum cleaner's dust bag. "Then the ray gun and after that the treasure (thinking of the fly spray and the sunlit dust.) Then the moon-mad-merry-go-round and the warm sleeping place (that was the electric egg beater and the oven. And then the sword! (that was the knife.)

"But I did some real haunting at last — oh yes — real haunting and scared them all. 'Boo!' I cried, and *they* all cried, 'A ghost! A ghost!' "

That night someone picked up the book of ghost stories and opened at the very page the ghost loved best — the one with a picture of a haunted house on it. The ghost flew in at the door of the haunted house and looked out from behind the curtain of the haunted window. "Home again!" it said. "That's the best place for a small ghost. Small but dangerous," it added. "Quite capable of doing a bit of haunting when it wants to."

Then the book was closed and the very small ghost went to sleep.

Plans Gone Wrong

On the edge of the well sat the wicked king.
He lifted his voice and began to sing:

"However wicked I've been before
I'm going to be wicked again and more.

"A hundred kingdoms shall be mine.
I'll wash their streets with blood and wine.

"A thousand cities shall bow and weep.
Their scrambling people shall die like sheep.

"On the gates of the sky my name shall ring,
And I shall be king, king, king, king, KING!"

That's what the wicked king sang as he sat
Planning the wickedness he would be at.

But he slipped as he sang and he drowned in the well.
You never can tell! You never can tell!

Green Marmalade to You

There was once a boy called Clutha who lived
with a cat and a crocodile and they were very
happy together. The strange thing was that each
of them spoke a different language from the
other two so that ordinary conversation was full
of guesses and question marks. However,
mostly they understood each other very well.

One day they all got up together and each one
of them opened his bedroom door at exactly the
same time as the other two.

"Good morning," said Clutha.

"Gone mooning," said the cat.

"Green marmalade!" cried the crocodile.

(But they all meant the same thing really.)

"It's a lovely day, isn't it?" called Clutha.

"It's a lively doe, isn't it?" observed the cat.

"Ladylike Ding-Dong!" exclaimed the
crocodile, putting up its blue frilly sunshade to
prove it.

(But, as you will have guessed they all meant the same thing really.)

Now the problem was to find something they all liked for breakfast. Clutha wanted porridge, and the cat said he wanted chops (though he may have meant chips.) As for the crocodile, it couldn't choose between cheese and cherries so they decided to have something totally different.

"How about bacon and eggs?" asked Clutha.
"Very tasty bacon and eggs!"

"Break–in and exit! Very toasty!" agreed the
cat.

"Broken explosions. Very twisty!" the
crocodile concurred twirling its blue sunshade.

So they had broken explosions for breakfast
and they enjoyed them very much. But after

breakfast there is always a problem, as you
know. Dirty dishes!

"We'd better do the washing up, I suppose,"
said Clutha.

"We'd batter down the swishing cup,"
nodded the cat.

"Buttered clown is wishing out," finished the
crocodile — or it sounded like that.

So they did the dishes and then they went out
to play.

Now, maybe one green marmalade you'll
wake up on a ladylike ding-dong and have
broken explosions for breakfast too — you'll
find them very twisty! But don't forget to
butter the clown and swish the cup when you
do the wishing out, will you?

The Flingamango

Oh the wily flingamango
Is a very agile bird
He can dance a pretty tango
Though his foxtrot is absurd.

In a ballet dress of paper
He will whirl for half the night
Sending those who see him caper,
Into Transports of Delight.

Frightening the Monster in Wizard's Hole

One day a truck load of bricks went over a
bump and two bricks fell off into the middle of
the road. They lay there like two new laid
oblong eggs, dropped by some unusual bird. A
boy called Tom-Tom coming down the road
stopped to look at them. He picked one up. It
was a beautiful glowing orange coloured brick
and it seemed as if it should be used for something special, but what can you do that's special
with only one brick or even two.

"Hey Tom-Tom!" called his friend Sam
Bucket coming up behind him. "What are you
doing with that brick?"

"Just holding it," Tom-Tom said, "holding it
and thinking . . . ."

"Thinking what?"

" . . . thinking that I'd take it and throw it really hard at . . ."

"At whom, Tom-Tom?"

"At the monster in Wizard's Hole."

Sam's eyes and mouth opened like early morning windows. "You'd be too scared."

"No I wouldn't! That's what I'm going to do now."

Tom-Tom set off down the road with his bright orange brick. Sam Bucket did not see why Tom-Tom should have all the glory and adventure. He grabbed the brick that was left in the middle of the road.

"Hang on Tom-Tom! I'm coming too."

"Okay!" said Tom-Tom grandly. "But don't forget it's my idea, so I'm going to throw first."

"Where're you two off to?" asked a farmer leaning over his gate.

"We're going to throw these bricks at the monster in Wizard's Hole," explained Tom-Tom.

"He's going to throw first and I'm going to throw next," cried Sam boastfully.

"You'd never dare!" cried the farmer.

"We're on our way now," they said together, strutting like bantam roosters along the sunny dusty road.

"But how are you going to get the monster out of Wizard's Hole?" asked the farmer. "He hasn't looked out for years."

"I shall shout at him," declared Tom-Tom grandly. "I shall say, 'Come on, Monster, out you come!' and he'll have to come, my voice will be so commanding."

"I shall shout too," said Sam Bucket quickly. " 'Come out, Monster,' I shall say. 'Come out and have bricks thrown at you.' My voice will be like a lion's roar. He'll have to come."

"Hang on a moment," said the farmer. "I've got a brick down here for holding my gate open. I'm coming too."

Off went Tom-Tom, Sam Bucket and the farmer, all holding bricks, all marching with a sense of purpose. They passed Mrs Puddenytame's Pumpkin farm. Mrs Puddenytame herself was out subduing the wild twining pumpkins.

"You lot look pleased with yourselves," she remarked as they went by.

"We are," said Tom-Tom, "because we're on our way to do great things. You see these bricks? We're on our way to throw them at the monster in Wizard's Hole."

"You'd never dare!" breathed Mrs Puddenytame. "Why, they say that the monster is all lumpy and bumpy, horrible, hairy and hideous — and besides, he hasn't bothered anyone for a hundred years."

"He's there, isn't he?" asked Sam Bucket. " 'Come out,' we'll say, 'out you come, Monster, and have bricks thrown at you."

"He'll have to come," cried the farmer. "And when he feels our bricks he'll run like a rabbit. We'll be heroes to the whole country."

"Well, hang on then!" Mrs Puddenytame shouted. "I've got a few spare bricks myself — and seven sons too." And she hunted the sons out of the pumpkins shouting, "Come on you louts! You can be heroes too."

"But mother," said her eldest, cleverest son, "nobody else wants Wizard's Hole. Why shouldn't the monster stay there?"

"He's a monster isn't he?" yelled Mrs Puddenytame. "Who ever heard of rights for monsters. You get a brick and come along with the

rest of us." Off they went, eleven people all carrying bricks down the sunny dusty road to town.

Once they got to town people came out of their houses to watch them. People followed them down the road. There was quite a procession by the time they reached the town square

with the fountain in the middle of it. There
Tom–Tom made a speech.

"Friends," he cried, "the time has come to
act. We are going to throw bricks at the monster in Wizard's Hole."

"We're going to roar like lions," added Sam
Bucket.

"And stamp like bulls!" agreed the farmer
stamping.

"We're going to laugh like hyenas, and shriek
like mad parrots," Mrs Puddenytame shouted,
"and frighten the monster into the next country. We've had the monster for too long. Let
someone else have him."

"Hooray!" shouted all the people.

"The monster will run . . . ." promised
Tom–Tom.

"He'll flee!" agreed Sam Bucket.

"He'll fly!" gloated the farmer.

"He'll bound and pound and turn head over head over heels!" declared Mrs Puddenytame weighing her brick in her hand.

"I think I'll get a brick too," said the mayor thoughtfully, looking at a truckload of bricks parked by a building construction site. "Nothing should be done without a mayor."

"Don't forget the school children!" cried an anxious teacher. "Remember they're the citizens of tomorrow."

"But what are we doing it for?" asked a small child surprised.

"For the good of the community. Go and find a brick," commanded the teacher.

Soon everyone had a taken a brick from the back of the truck and was marching sternly towards Wizard's Hole.

The monster was just sitting down to a breakfast of fried eggs and crisp bacon when he heard
the sound of many feet marching towards his
front door.

"Visitors — at last!" thought the monster. He
rushed to his bed cave, put on a collar and tie,
washed behind his ears and brushed his many
teeth. Then he ran to his front door and put his
head out of Wizard's Hole.

"Good morning!" he said and smiled.
Everyone stopped. Tom-Tom stopped, Sam
Bucket stopped. The farmer, Mrs Puddenytame
and her seven sons, the mayor and the school
teacher — everyone stopped.

"Come on in . . . I'm just making fresh
coffee." The monster smiled again showing his
newly brushed teeth. He had a lot of teeth, this
monster, many of them green and all of them
sharp. Everyone stared.

"Do come in. I'm so pleased to see you," wheedled the monster. But the monster was wheedling in monster language which is a mixture of growling, whining, roaring and shrieking. Every single person dropped his brick. Every single solitary person ran without looking back once.

"Goodness me!" said the monster looking at the bricks. "Are all these presents for me? Too kind! Too kind! Thank you . . ." he called after them. But he said the Thank-you in monster language which is a mixture of rumbling, snarling and screaming. Everyone ran even faster than ever before.

The monster went in and put on his bricklayer's apron, got his bricklayer's trowel and made himself a handsome brick monster house. Then he moved out of Wizard's Hole which had always been so damp that the wallpaper peeled off, and he lived happily ever after.

And when Tom-Tom heard what had happened he said: "Well, we got him out of Wizard's Hole any way."

And felt very successful.

The Star-Crossed Lovers

"Oh, do you remember, my darling . . . . ?"
"I cannot remember," said he,
"But was I a succulent starling
When you were the leaf on a tree?

"And then I turned into a trumpet
And you were the music I played.
And was I a hot buttered crumpet
When you were some fresh marmalade?

120

"I know I have met with you often
But cannot remember the place.
I was once an astrologer's coffin
And you were the smile on his face.

"We're acquainted but never together.
We encounter but never unite,
For I was a spell of bad weather
When you were a Saturday night.

"Are we dice that the devil is tossing?
Are we never permitted to choose?
I was once a pedestrian crossing
When you were a pair of old shoes.

"Both bound by a singular star, still
Our places in space don't agree,
For I am a conjuror's castle
And you are a cake for his tea."

The Silly Song

Hey ding a ding,
Hey ding a dong,
Life is so silly,
And so is this song.

A telegraph pole is immensely absurd.
It stands on one leg like a sort of bird.
It stands on one leg and pretends it's not there,
While workers on ladders are plaiting its hair.

Hey ding a ding,
Hey ding a dong,
Life is so silly,
And so is this song.

The very tall houses they're building these days
Have their toes in the town and their heads in a haze.
You go up in a lift and incredibly soon
You can knock on the door of the man in the moon.

    Hey ding a ding,
    Hey ding a dong,
    Life is so silly
    And so is this song.

There's nothing as mad as the cars in the street.
They trundle on wheels where they ought to have feet.
But if they had feet they would only get corns
And then they'd start grumbling and blowing their
horns.

Hey ding a ding,
Hey ding a dong.
Life is so silly,
And so is this song.

The telegraph poles and the houses and cars
May sing the same song that is sung by the stars,
But if ever I start such a wonderful song
It always comes out as a Hey ding a dong.

Hey ding a ding,
Hey ding a dong,
Life is so silly,
And so is this song.